DIBUJAR

ESPACIOS

María Oñorbe Gómez

Rivers of Ink

europa
ediciones

© 2025 **Europa Ediciones** | Madrid
www.grupoeditorialeuropa.es

ISBN 9791256960880
I edición: junio del 2025
Distribuidor para las librerías: **CAL Málaga S.L.**

Impreso para Italia por *Rotomail Italia S.p.A. - Vignate (MI)*
Stampato in Italia presso *Rotomail Italia S.p.A. - Vignate (MI)*

Rivers of Ink

For all the teenagers who left home to find home: I hope your heart is healing well.

"She took all that she felt,
all the love, all the risk,
and from the tip of her pen,
streamed rivers of ink."

Contents

PROLOGUE..*13*

Poet's notes: Feelings...*15*

Fell in love...*17*

Not a Fairy Tale..*20*

I hate that I like you...*22*

will you miss me?..*25*

Math Class...*28*

Risking my life..*30*

do you wanna…?..*32*

NUNCA..*34*

miedo..*36*

just US..*38*

stupid..*39*

Gn...*41*

That other girl..*43*

Grizzlies vs. Bucks..*45*

"Solo amigos" *47*

"Everything"...*49*

Love..*52*

…again? *55*

BLUE *57*

Pretty *59*

home 61

NOT in love...63

Ursa Major..64

the act 66

Senseless (and stupid) arguments...................68

Valor..70

She's my friend 72

My Freshman Girl 74

Bad Girl..76

Eres precioso 78

The Golden Rule 81

121...83

A Tan Solo Cinco Días.............................84

¿Qué me has hecho?...............................86

Goodbyes suck 88

It Hurts That I Can't Hate You...................90

There's a place 92

An Empty chair 94

VOID..95

Remember US 96

Always best friends 98

4130 miles 100

Sixteen..102

AKNOWLEDGEMENTS 105

PROLOGUE

Rivers of ink is a collection of poems in which the author shows all the wonder, the beauty, the poignant depth of a feeling, love, that gives life even when it causes pain, when it is tormented, unrequited, silent.

Each poem explores love by highlighting a different facet of it. The author, with her young age, shows us how loving can be easy and complicated at the same time. The poems follow the various steps of falling in love, each describing the emotional toll it takes:

«[…] *Fell in love with the love./Fell in love with the hate./And, although it was rough,/fell in love with the pain.*» 'Fell in Love'

«[…] *So I guess that what I'm saying/is that I'm afraid of you,/because you will never like me/and I hate that I like you.*» 'I hate that I like you'

«[…] *The problem is that I'm delusional,/the problem is that I don't care,/that I knew it was impossible/and, no matter what, I fell.*» 'Risking my life'

«[…] *NUNCA pensé que una mirada/pudiera decir más que mil palabras/y aquí estás tú, y yo confundida/porque tus ojos me gritan que entre en tu vida.*» 'NUNCA'

The style is simple and delicate; the vocabulary bare and essential, devoid of elements that could shift the focus to anything other than the sentiment itself. Among the various rhetorical figures, anaphora (*Home, Fell in love, Nunca*) and alliteration («*[…] It hurts to think I opened up/and that you left me on read,/it hurts to think there was an 'us'/and that I thought we were friends»* In 'It hurts that I can't hate you'; «*[…] Cause there's a place that's in my mind,/in my memories, my heart,/it's a place I left behind.../and I wish I could go back»* In 'There's a place') are prominent.

The presence of poems in Spanish makes the collection even more poignant and romantic, emphasising even more how love can be a feeling that can make one suffer but can also heal.

POET'S NOTE: FEELINGS

Being a teenager is… complicated. Teenagers feel twice as much as anyone else, intensely, with passion. A dumb crush can feel like the love of your life, and a heartbreak seems to be the end of the world. We can be surrounded by people and still be the loneliest person in the world. Quite often, we feel like we don't have anyone who understands us, who has felt this way before. We can even think that there's no one they can cry to without being weak, or sensitive.

This is how I felt for a very long time. I just turned sixteen and, in the past five months, I have felt more than I ever thought possible: pain, love, happiness, doubts, nostalgia, sadness, and fear. Lots of fear. Because, yeah, being a teenager is complicated, but being a teenager in a completely new country, all by yourself? That is terrifying. But it's also the most beautiful thing ever. It's sad and magical and wonderful. It's everything. And, just like life itself when you are fifteen years old, it can feel so, so, so… lonely.

In my case, all these emotions (all the pain, the love, the happiness, the doubts, the fear, the nostalgia, the sadness, the loneliness…) created an artist. Because I know that leaving your home can be hard, especially when you feel everything so intensely, and because I know that having someone who feels the same way can be the most healing thing ever. Because I don't want anyone to feel like they are not heard, not seen, not felt. So, I took all those ideas and all those experiences, whether personal little things or universal feelings, and used them to create flowing rivers that streamed from my pen and into the pages of my little notebook. Rivers of fear, love, sadness and happiness… Rivers of Ink.

FELL IN LOVE

Fell in love, not with a girl.
Fell in love, not with a boy.
'Cause when I forgot the pain
I fell so hard for the joy.

Fell in love with an illusion.
Fell in love with a mirage.
Or maybe this is the conclusion
to all my broken hearts.

Fell in love with a feeling.
Fell in love with a song.
Fell in love with believing
nothing else would go wrong.

Fell in love with trying.
Fell in love with books.
Fell in love with writing
and with living out my youth.

Fell in love with a story.

Fell in love with the dark.

It all used to feel blurry,

but now I see the sun.

Fell in love with every new thing.

Fell in love with every smile.

Fell in love with just existing.

Fell in love with running wild.

Fell in love with the happiness.

Fell in love with the fear.

Fell in love with the sadness,

'cause it meant I would heal.

Fell in love with the love.

Fell in love with the hate.

And, although it was rough,

fell in love with the pain.

Fell in love with my family.

Fell in love with my friends.

Fell in love with strangers.

Fell in love with myself.

Fell in love with the ashes.

Fell in love with the fire.

Fell in love with my madness…

I fell in love with my life

NOT A FAIRY TALE

Once upon a time…

I don't think that's how to start.

I'd be telling you a lie,

this didn't happen in the past.

Right now, sat on a couch,

there's a girl who dreams of you,

who looks for you in the crowd

and believes that you do, too.

And she knows she is make-believing.

Sure, she knows that you're not hers,

but she likes to keep pretending

that she'll wake to see you there.

For her you have a hundred faces

of all the people that she's liked;

sometimes you look like that black-haired girl

or like that boy with the blue eyes.

Yeah, for her, you're just a fantasy,

you're a dream that won't come true.

You're a smile when no one's watching

and a "great, what about you?"

And though she knows that she won't find you,

that doesn't mean that she won't try.

Oh, true love, how would have I known

that you'd be so, so hard to find?

I HATE THAT I LIKE YOU

I think now I understand

what Taylor meant in So High School

and I hate it so, so much.

Oh, and, why? 'Cause you're a damn fool.

'Cause all night, I waited up,

just thinking bout the two of us,

but then we barely talk in class

and you flirt only through Snaps.

You make me feel like a teenager

everytime I get your texts.

I know I'm only a tenth grader,

but I thought I was the best.

I really thought that I was past that,

really thought I wouldn't fall,

but I blush when I open Snapchat

and when I see you in the hall.

I really wish that I could tell you

all the things you make me feel

and I really wish that you knew

that your eyes cut deep through me.

I also wish that I was braver,

that I could gather up my strength,

just to ask you, dear stranger,

if you remember my name.

Because yours has been in my mind

every minute since we met.

Oh, that smile, and those big blue eyes

will surely take me to my grave!

And I just wanna know about you,

about your fears and your dreams.

I would text you at all hours

and hope that you asked about me.

But, then again, what would I tell you?

I'm afraid you'd run away.

If you asked me about what I do,

I don't know what I would say.

'Cause the girl that you have talked with…,

she's not even half of me.

She didn't tell you she likes reading

or that she really loves to speak.

So I guess that what I'm saying

is that I'm afraid of you,

because you will never like me

and I hate that I like you.

WILL YOU MISS ME?

never thought that i could fall,
but i have, in what a way!
i keep staring at my phone,
waiting for you to say "hey"

but, i mean, how could i not?
it's as if you were made for me.
i kinda think that you come from
somewhere beyond my wildest dreams.

my friends keep feeding up my hope,
they say you're perfect for me.
i'm so scared of getting lost
and yet i'm into you, deep.

"he's for sure flirting with you",
that is what my best friend said
when i asked him if he knew
why you were acting that way.

but then you suddenly ignore me,

you don't answer to my texts.

it's almost like you have forgotten,

like you've left me on a shelf.

and i don't wanna let you go,

don't wanna let you go away,

but i feel like you'll be gone,

feel like you'll do it anyway.

and i can barely remember

who i am, when i'm with you.

i really hope it will get better,

i also guess i will get through.

that doesn't mean that you don't hurt me,

it doesn't mean that i'm not down,

it only means that, at some point, i…

i won't feel like i do now.

and maybe that day you will miss me,

maybe i will miss you, too.

'cause my friends know that i've never

felt the way i feel for you.

MATH CLASS

Today's Math was like a daydream,
one I don't wanna wake up from;
met all these people, all these strangers
and their smiles were true and warm.

Today in Math I heard your laughter,
you were laughing 'cause of me.
You asked me to speak in Spanish
and I almost couldn't breathe.

Today's Math was just so weird,
but so perfect all the same.
Yeah, I can barely believe it,
but I met all of your friends.

Today in Math… you must've been kidding,
'cause I died when you said my name!
I was flying, I was feeling
like you were all that is okay.

Today's Math was just a fantasy,

but it was real, wasn't it?

Well, it still doesn't feel like it,

it's like I'm living a dream.

And even though I get this feeling

that it won't happen again,

today in Math we weren't faking:

today in Math, you were my friend

RISKING MY LIFE

I didn't fall, I guess I jumped,
I dived headfirst into you,
and I know when I hit the land
I'm gonna get a quite bad bruise.

And all of my friends have warned me
about having this dumb crush.
They have told me you mean problems
and I should run now that I can.

But I'm afraid that I can't do it,
that it's already too late,
that it's just me who I'm fooling
when I say that I'm okay.

'Cause your name hits like a bullet
that is aimed right to my heart
and the way all my friends put it,
you're gonna hit so hard.

You've already let me down
even though I barely know you
and, with all that I know now,
I feel like I shouldn't want to…

the problem is, I really do,
I wanna know it all 'bout you:
all your fears, all your dreams,
all the things I shouldn't wish.

I could burn or I could drown,
honestly, I couldn't care less,
'cause whenever you're around
I'm this godforsaken mess.

You're the fire, you're the water
and I'm the only one I'm blaming.
I'm the lamb, you are the slaughter.
You're the risk that I am taking.

DO YOU WANNA…?

All my friends have warned me,

they've told me that you're bad,

they've told me that you'll hurt me

and that then you'll break my heart.

But the problem isn't you,

at least that is what I think.

'Cause I know I'm such a fool

and I know the problem's me.

The problem is that I'm delusional,

the problem is that I don't care,

that I knew it was impossible

and, no matter what, I fell.

Though I don't think the problem was falling for you.

No, my problem was always thinking you would,

that I stood a chance between all those girls,

that you would choose me at the end of the day.

And I guess it'd be easier not going insane

if your eyes and the sea did not look the same;

I guess it'd be easier not looking at you

if I didn't know that you look at me, too.

So decide what you choose,

darling, make up your mind.

I'm waiting for you;

do you wanna be mine?

NUNCA

NUNCA había admirado el color del cielo…

hasta que llegaste tú; tus ojos, su reflejo.

NUNCA pensé que me ahogaría en el mar,

pero veo ese azul y quiero saltar.

NUNCA he creído en sentir mariposas,

pero aparecen al ver esa sonrisa en tu boca.

NUNCA creí que un dios existiera,

pero veo tu rostro y no hay otra manera.

NUNCA pensé que una mirada

pudiera decir más que mil palabras

y aquí estás tú, y yo confundida

porque tus ojos me gritan que entre en tu vida.

NUNCA pensé que, en tan solo un día,

podía mirarte y caer rendida,

pero me hablaste una vez, no más que una

y, desde entonces, me encuentro en la Luna.

Y dije que NUNCA me enamoraría,

que tan solo unos meses y te olvidaría.

Dije que un "nosotros" NUNCA funcionaría…

y eso es lo único que creo todavía.

Nunca, nunca, NUNCA diré que te quería,

en cambio mis amigas me oirán todos los días

gritándoles que odio la manera en que me miras.

Y tú nunca, nunca, NUNCA sabrás que son mentiras.

MIEDO

Creo que nunca había sentido

tanto miedo de caer,

aunque sé que ya he caído

y no se puede deshacer.

Y tal vez es tu sonrisa,

que me acelera el corazón,

o la forma en que me miras,

que hace que pierda la razón.

Tal vez es cómo me hablas,

que siempre me haces reír,

tal vez es que me das largas

y no me quieres escribir.

Tal vez es que me he dado cuenta,

que he empezado a percibir,

que, cuando me doy la vuelta,

tus ojos están en mí.

Tal vez es porque contigo
se me van todas las dudas,
tal vez es porque he entendido
que a tu lado estoy segura.

Pero el caso es que te quiero,
y me da miedo quererte;
y me da mucho más miedo
que me da miedo perderte.

JUST US

Just one smile, just one look.

That's the story: I like you.

Just one stupid question…, no one could tell

that I looked in your eyes and instantly fell.

There was just you,

there was just me.

Nobody I knew,

at least until I did.

Now I guess there's just us,

though it doesn't exist

because I fell for you,

but did you fall for me?

STUPID

I don't think that you are stupid,
that's my answer to your question.
Oh, how could I, now that Cupid
has made you draw my attention?

But I do think that you are kind,
that you're cute and really nice.
I also think that you're so tall
and that I love it when we talk.

Yeah, I think you've got that smile…,
or maybe that look in your eyes…,
but there's something about you
that makes me wanna tell the truth.

And the truth is: I like you,
oh my God, I really do
and I kinda wish you knew,
although I am quite scared, too.

Cause I don't think you feel that way

and I guess that it's okay,

but I can't help thinking, someday,

maybe you will feel the same.

And in three months I'll be gone

and you'll probably forget me…

Going back to where I'm from

hasn't ever felt so scary.

So I guess that you could find me,

though it's only a suggestion.

No, I don't think that you're stupid,

that's my answer to your question.

GN

There's times when I hate myself
more than I could ever love me.
God, I'm so stupid, and I swear
that it's not because I'm foreign!

It's cause I believed your friends
when they told me that you liked me;
cause I chose to think you cared,
when I knew that we were nothing.

It's cause I was so damn sure
that I meant something to you;
it's cause now I see I don't
and, yet, I still care a lot.

It's cause I still think of Saturday,
when you sent me a "good night" text...
It's been just forty-eight hours
and we're strangers again.

It's because it is my fault

that we don't talk anymore.

It's because I kinda know

that you don't miss me, not at all.

THAT OTHER GIRL

Of course there's another girl
and I guess I should've known that.
Now I am so damn afraid
that she'll be just what you want and

I haven't even met her,
no, I don't know who she is,
but I wish that I could be her
or that she was more like me.

Yeah, I bet that she's so pretty,
that she's funny and so smart…
Oh, I bet she has you feeling
like she just stole your heart.

And I hope that she can love you
almost as much as I did
'cause I want you to be happy,
even if it's not with me.

There's so much I wanna tell you,

but I guess I'm way too scared,

so you won't know that I'm so blue

'cause I know I can't be her.

GRIZZLIES VS. BUCKS

Today I wore my Grizzlies jersey,
you were wearing your Bucks sweatshirt.
You looked at me, then turned away,
but, in a moment, glanced again.

And I couldn't help but laughing
at the awkward situation,
cause your eyes did all the talking,
though I don't know if they meant to.

By the way, Memphis is winning
tonight's game and many more!
Know you don't think they're a good team,
but who cares? I surely don't.

That concerns me, cause I'd never
let someone mess with the Grizz.
Yet you have and now, however,
I want you to talk to me.

Cause we argued about basket

when we should've gone to sleep;

I was laying on the carpet,

waiting for you to text me.

And I like you anyway,

even though I hate your team…

So, it's Memphis or Milwaukee,

but one of us has to win.

"SOLO AMIGOS"

Y dijimos "solo amigos",
pero no sé si es así,
porque cuando estoy contigo
solo puedo sonreír.

Y dijimos "solo amigos",
aunque sabes que te quiero…
Negaré que me has herido,
aunque eso no sea cierto.

Pero no puedo culparte
porque no sientas lo mismo;
en verdad, tengo que amarte
por ser tan bueno conmigo,

por decir que soy amable,
que podemos ser amigos…
¿Por qué elegiste quedarte
si podrías haberte ido?

Y como sé que tu deseo

es que seamos "solo amigos",

me callaré, aunque no creo

que hagan falta más testigos.

Porque, si te soy sincera,

¿la manera en que te miro?

Ay, cariño, aunque me duela…,

así no miro a mis amigos.

Pero en eso hemos quedado,

en que somos "solo amigos".

Diré que te he superado,

aunque aún sueño contigo.

"EVERYTHING"

When I asked: "What do you know?",
you said: "Everything". But you don't.
You don't know everything, there is no way,
cause there's so much I didn't say.

I didn't say it cause I couldn't,
couldn't put it into words.
Oh, I couldn't, at least not in
any language you would know.

Cause I could tell you que te quiero,
but I don't think you'd understand.
I could tell you: "tengo miedo;
no me quiero enamorar."

I could tell you que no puedo
dejar de pensar en ti.
I could tell you todo esto
and you'd not know what it means.

All the things I wanna tell you

seem to get stuck in my tongue.

Quiero que sepas que te quiero,

but I just can't find the words.

And the truth is, language barriers?

They seem pretty real now.

¿Cómo hago que me ames

if I can't say it out loud?

So you don't know everything, you just can't;

you know so little, not even half

of all the things I feel for you,

all the things I wish you knew:

que te quiero, casi te amo,

no me quería enamorar,

pero cada vez que hablamos

te quiero un poquito más;

que ojalá tú me quisieras,

aunque sé que no lo harás.

I could tell you all I feel and…

and you wouldn't understand.

LOVE

There was a time,

some years ago,

when all my life

was without love.

I felt betrayed,

I felt so lost,

I had nowhere

I could call home.

Oh, at that time

I really thought

that I'd be fine

all on my own.

But I grew up,

I found some friends,

I found my path…

I smiled again.

And now I'm happy,

of course I am,

but there is one thing

I wish I had.

And it's there, in every movie

and in every book I read;

something that I never needed

until, suddenly, I did.

I also see it in my friends,

in the way they talk and laugh;

it feels like it never ends

(I love to think it never does).

And I've felt it, but I've never

been loved back by anyone,

at this point, it'd be quite clever

to assume that I just can't.

I can't be loved back, I'm too much,

I fall in love with all my heart;

so I'm still waiting for the one,

for the one who'll hold my hand.

Because that love is a dream,

something I can only think of,

that some lucky get to live…

while the rest survive without love.

…AGAIN?

I thought that I was over you,
I promise you, I was…
Or maybe that is not true,
maybe I was still down bad.

But I do think that I did it:
I stopped thinking about you.
The problem is that all those feelings
came back sooner than they should.

Cause when the coldness turned to smiles
and the joking became "thank you"s,
when the nice words melted the ice…
I think that is when I fell through.

Not sure when, but all the chatting
became a pretty common thing.
All the smiles, the looks, the laughing…
You're someone you'd never been.

And now I can't bring myself

to stop thinking about you,

about all the things you said,

about all the things you do.

BLUE

There is no way that you'll like me,

that's why I got over you,

but these weeks you have been nicer…

and your eyes are still bright blue.

Yeah, your eyes are still bright blue,

that deep blue that I could drown in…

Ever since we met, I knew

that this would be a disaster.

Cause I never loved the sea

and I never loved the sky…

I didn't love what was to see

until I saw it in your eyes.

I never loved the color blue,

but now I see it all around me;

and it was when I met you

that it began to feel like magic.

Yeah, the blue was just a color,

just the one the Grizzlies wore…,

but since I met you there's another

deeper meaning to the word.

Blue's the color of the logo

of that tee you always wear,

blue's the background of that photo

in which you look so damn well.

Blue's the color of your eyes,

of those eyes I fell in love with…,

and feeling blue will be the price,

because I shouldn't have fallen.

PRETTY

I'm not pretty,

I know I'm not,

I came to terms with it

years ago...,

but sometimes I wish I was,

I kinda wish I could believe it,

cause I hate each single thought

that comes to mind when I see me.

I hate that I can't stand my hair,

which all my friends say that they love;

I hate that I can't see myself

without thinking "not enough".

I hate that I look at those girls

full of jealousy and envy,

straight hair or perfect curls...,

but they all look so much better.

I hate that sometimes I feel pretty,

but then I realize I'm not.

I'm not pretty, how could I be

when those girls are all so hot?

HOME

I left my home, cried on the plane.
"I'll be alone, I have no friends."
Then I got here and it all changed:
I met my people, I found my place.

Cause all these people made me smile,
they made me happy, healed me inside,
and though I know this life's not mine
there's things it'll hurt to leave behind.

And all my family, all my friends
say "I can't wait to see you again"
and I miss them, but I'm afraid…
I wish that day just never came.

It's not that I don't miss my people,
it's not that I don't miss my home…
It's just that now I found this feeling
and I don't want it to be gone.

It's just that I love all this people,

that they're now my second home…

and I'm so scared that if I leave 'em

they'll forget me, cause I won't.

NOT IN LOVE

When my friend said "you're in love,"

I quickly answered "no, I'm not.

I'm not in love, how could I be?"

"It's just the way you talk bout him…"

And I don't think she understands

how much I need that to be false,

because I know I'm not in love…,

but I'm not that sure anymore.

URSA MAJOR

First night in the USA,
I felt such a real, deep pain,
cause I looked up at the night sky
and I could not believe my eyes.

I couldn't see her in the dark,
couldn't find her in the stars,
for the first time, she wasn't there;
I could not see the Great Bear.

And I had never paid attention
(she was just a constellation),
but she had watched me all my life,
she'd always lit up my sky.

She was a symbol of my home,
that I left for a couple months,
of all the things I left behind…
Somehow this felt like a sign.

So I looked up at the starred sky

for some weeks, each single night,

till I finally got to know them;

all those stars now gave me light.

And the Great Bear wasn't there,

I had grown up next to her…,

but I learnt to love these stars,

it was really easy, in fact.

And, just like that, my sky was lit

by all those stars I'd never seen.

My constellations shine so bright…

I'm scared of leaving them behind.

These new stars have made me feel

happier than I'd ever been.

And though the Great Bear is not there…,

I found all of them instead.

THE ACT

Yeah, we're just friends, of course we are,
but when you smile at me like that…
No! We're just friends… Oh, I could laugh,
but I'll just keep up with the act.

Cause I can tell a hundred lies,
but that won't make it more real;
I can fall for different guys
who will never make me feel that.

I can pretend that nothing happens,
pretend there's nothing going on,
but I can feel it in the silence
and in my words each time we talk.

I'll keep on acting like your smile
doesn't tear down all my walls,
I'll keep on acting all my life
if that means that you won't go.

Cause I just love you way too much

and I'm not willing to risk it.

So we're just friends, not more than that…

though I kinda wish you'd kiss me.

SENSELESS (AND STUPID) ARGUMENTS

Tell me whatever you want,

try and prove me that you're right,

cause even when I know you're wrong

if you say it with that smile…

And it's true that I won't listen,

there's no way to change my mind,

but I'm thinking and there isn't

any reason not to try.

It's not that I just wanna see you,

that I wanna talk to you,

that I need to find a reason

to turn around and look at you.

Not that I wanna see that smile

that appears when I get mad,

not that it gives me butterflies

when you look at me like that.

Of course I didn't spend the night
looking for ways to prove you wrong,
looking for ways to start a fight
or for ways to piss you off.

It's not that I just love an argument
if I'm arguing with you.
It's just that I know about basket
and it looks like you do, too.

Yeah, of course that I hate arguing
and of course I hate you, too…
except that you know that I'm lying
and that I love to talk to you.

VALOR

Me encantaría ser valiente,

ojalá tener valor

para decir directamente

que me has robado el corazón.

Que ahora tengo tu sonrisa

grabada a fuego en mi mente.

Que la forma en que me miras

hace que no importe la gente.

Que me encanta cómo hablas,

y tu forma de reír,

que me faltan las palabras

cuando tú estás junto a mí.

Y es que tú no te das cuenta,

no pareces percibir

que, cuando te das la vuelta,

yo solo te miro a ti.

Y es que cuando estoy contigo

vuelvo a sentir mariposas

porque aunque somos "solo amigos",

yo te veo como otra cosa.

Pero no puedo decirlo

porque tengo mucho miedo

de que sepas que he caído,

de que sepas que te quiero.

SHE'S MY FRIEND

I think I need to force myself
to stop thinking about you
because you like someone else
—and I kinda already knew.

But now that I know her name,
that I know the way she looks,
that I know that she's my friend…
Now I know what I must do.

Cause I could've ruined our friendship
and I didn't really care,
but now I'm not willing to risk it
because now I know it's her.

And it might hurt for some minutes,
maybe for a couple months,
but I know that all these feelings,
at some point, will finally go.

And I'll always have the memory
of our chatting and your smile,
but I'm OK with just memories
if I have her by my side.

MY FRESHMAN GIRL

Smiles that we shared during classes,

all the chatting in the halls,

the tea-spilling during science

(we never get any work done).

All the things that I have told you

and the way that you react,

those little comments I'll hold on to

when we only talk through chat.

Science homework that I sent you

and the facetimes late at night.

I don't think I got to tell you,

but nobody shines so bright.

I hope you know I'm gonna miss you,

hope you know I'm gonna cry

when I think about what I'd do

if I had you by my side.

But there's an ocean in between us,

we're four thousand miles apart,

so I guess I'll have to miss you

till the day that I come back.

BAD GIRL

I kinda wish that I could smile
at a thousand different people,
that I could say that they're fine
without ever catching feelings.

And, for once, I think I'd like
to just try and be the bad girl,
to be the one that leaves behind
a little trail of people crying.

Yeah, for once, I'd really love
to just break somebody's heart,
to be pretty, maybe known,
to just be somebody's crush.

Cause, for once, it would be nice
if I could maybe be that girl,
the kind of girl who doesn't cry
for someone she couldn't get.

The kind of girl who is not lonely,

who has people in her past,

the kind of girl whose phone is burning

with dms, and texts, and snaps.

The kind of girl who doesn't fall,

because people fall for her…

To be the poem, not the poet

who gave her heart to someone else.

ERES PRECIOSO

Eres precioso,

por dentro y por fuera,

y yo daría todo

porque tú lo supieras.

Y es que no eres consciente

de cómo sonríes,

de que se graba en mi mente

cada cosa que dices.

Porque no te das cuenta

de que quiero besarte,

de cómo me afecta

tenerte delante.

Y será el metro ochenta,

o tus ojos marrones,

pero, aunque no deba,

me he hecho ilusiones.

Y sé que, ¡dios no quiera!,
si nunca te vuelvo a ver,
pensaré en lo que era
y en lo que pudo ser.

Sé que te echaré de menos,
también sé que va a doler,
pero ya no me arrepiento
de atreverme a querer.

Porque te he querido a ti,
y me he sentido tan querida…
Me has enseñado a reír
y me has cambiado de por vida.

Así que, sí, eres precioso,
me has robado el corazón
y, cuando te miro a los ojos,
sé que hay una razón.

Porque quedan los recuerdos

de tus sonrisas, de reir,

de estar siempre en desacuerdo

y no parar de discutir.

Porque merece la pena

arriesgarme, si es por ti;

porque sé que, aunque me duela,

siempre vas a estar ahí.

Porque sé que me has querido,

aunque no como yo a ti;

porque hemos sido amigos

y me has hecho tan feliz…

THE GOLDEN RULE

There was just one golden rule:
don't get attached, just play it cool.
I know the "shoulds" and "shouldn't do"s,
but they don't work when it's 'bout you.

Cause I think I got too close
and now I'm scared to cut it loose,
cause I knew I had four months
and then I'd have to leave you.

Cause back then I didn't care,
four months seemed more than enough…,
but now I've got around ten days
and then I'll have to let you go.

Cause I can't live in love with someone
who lives one ocean apart,
but I already feel nostalgia
and I already want you back.

And it's funny cause I never,

not for a moment, had your heart

and, yet, mine is yours forever

(or at least this tiny part).

So you can keep it in a box,

or you can throw it to the sea,

but, please, promise that you won't

just go on and forget me.

There was just one golden rule:

don't fall in love, don't be a fool.

That stupid rule I said I knew…

but I forgot, cause it was you.

121

A hundred and twenty one days,

that's how long I had with you.

Now I wish that I could stay

because these days really flew.

A hundred and twenty one memories,

of the moments that I spent

next to you, of all this journey

that has now come to an end.

A hundred and twenty one people,

maybe you are even more,

that make me wish that I could stay here,

though I know I have to go.

A hundred and twenty one tears

that I've cried, cause I will leave.

A hundred and twenty one pieces

of my heart that will stay here.

A TAN SOLO CINCO DÍAS

Solo queda una semana,

y ya no te veré más

y tú ahora, de la nada,

te decides acercar.

Porque ahora me sonríes

y te sientas a mi lado,

hacemos bromas, tú te ríes

y se rozan nuestras manos.

Ahora hablamos todo el tiempo

y estoy cómoda contigo.

No te he dicho que te quiero,

aunque, tal vez, lo has entendido.

No sé si somos "solo amigos",

o si ahora hay algo más,

pero todos lo han sentido:

algo ha empezado a cambiar.

Pero en solo cinco días,

¿qué es lo que puedo hacer?

¿Qué más da si me querías

si nunca te vuelvo a ver?

¿QUÉ ME HAS HECHO?

Desde un primer momento

yo creía que eras guapo.

Ahora no sé lo que siento,

ni sé como ha pasado.

Porque de ser un gran amigo

has pasado a… no sé el qué,

pero quiero hablar contigo

y también te quiero ver.

Y sé que me voy en tres días

y no quiero cometer

otro error que dolería,

pero ya no sé qué hacer.

Sé que te voy a echar de menos,

eso lo he sabido siempre,

pero ahora creo que quiero

que me pidas que me quede.

Anoche, cuando me escribías,

cuando miraba los vídeos,

se me escapaba una sonrisa

y un sentimiento había surgido.

Y te he visto esta mañana

caminar por el pasillo

y me he puesto colorada,

se aceleraban mis latidos.

No sé muy bien lo que me has hecho,

pero no tiene sentido

que me gustes, porque quiero

que sigamos siendo amigos.

GOODBYES SUCK

Folding sweaters, closing bags,
and it kicked in, all at once:
I am leaving. And it's hard,
Cause I don't know when I'll be back.

And then, suddenly, I'm crying
on the floor of my bedroom,
and I'm crying during classes
and I even cry in church.

Cause I don't think I can do it,
I can't leave this place behind,
cause the things that I'll be losing
are the things that made me smile.

So now every time I cry,
I hope you know I cry for you,
cause I had to say goodbye
to all the people that I knew

who will soon become strangers,

though you said you'd miss me, too.

And soon I'll only have the memories

of four months I spent with you.

IT HURTS THAT I CAN'T HATE YOU

I know that I should probably hate you,

cause you hurt me so, so much,

but we both know that I'm not able

so I think I will give up.

But it hurts to think of you,

it hurts to think you lied to me,

cause you said you'd miss me too

and I just wanted to believe.

It hurts to think I opened up

and that you left me on read,

it hurts to think there was an "us"

and that I thought that we were friends.

But most of all, it hurts the way

in which I know this is not right,

but, man, I'd do it all again

and I'd believe each single lie.

Cause we both know that I'm not able

to treat you the way you deserve.

Yeah, you know I could never hate you,

no matter how much it will hurt.

THERE'S A PLACE

What they call "home" doesn't feel like it,
it's bringing tears to my eyes
and, though I know I should be smiling,
all I wanna do is cry.

Cause there's a place that's in my mind,
in my memories, my heart,
it's a place I left behind…
and I wish I could go back.

There's the people that I met there,
who I'll always think about,
and who, sadly I'm afraid I'll
have to learn to live without.

There's a school I'll always love,
that taught me how to be a human,
a school that now I call my own
though I know it's an illusion.

And I know I had to come home,

or at least that's what they said,

but it somehow still feels wrong,

like I never should've left.

AN EMPTY CHAIR

What exactly did you feel

when you saw my empty seat?

Were you happy? Were you sad?

Did you miss me during class?

Did my ghost sit on that chair?

Did you see her while she turned

around to you with a broad smile

or with tears in her eyes?

Did the memories of us

ponder your mind in our class?

Did you even think of me,

of the way it used to be?

Cause there's one thing I know for sure:

oh, I was thinking of you.

Did you miss me? I don't know…

Maybe you already forgot.

VOID

The sun shines, but I feel cold,
there's nothing that can bring me joy,
I'm so scared of getting old,
I feel trapped inside a void

of self-despair, of tears and fighting,
of hours crying in my room,
of hopeless feelings, of anxiety,
of wishing I was next to you.

Cause all the things I used to love
seem now empty, without meaning,
and I'm scared, down to my bones,
that I won't outgrow this feeling.

I'm so afraid that I will always
feel like I'm lost in my own life,
that I'm stuck, that there is no way
I'll be able to survive.

REMEMBER US

I hope you remember,

cause it hasn't left my head,

that 6th of September;

it was the day that I fell.

It only took one stupid question,

I think about it all the time,

how your voice caught my attention

and your words made my lips smile.

Our eyes met that afternoon,

you said "hi", I was down bad.

Just like that! I never knew

how to tell you what it was.

I also hope that you remember,

cause I can't let it go away,

one last month: that sweet December,

when you smiled at me again,

when we talked around the hallways

and spent classes lost in jokes,

when I really thought we'd always

be that close…, well, I was wrong.

But I hope that you remember

all the chatting and the laughs,

cause I keep holding on to memories

of a time when there was us.

ALWAYS BEST FRIENDS

Lately all I do is wonder
if I will ever go back,
if time will pass, if we'll get older…
I'm so scared we'll fall apart.

And I never thought it possible,
I could've never asked for this,
cause it has been truly awesome
having you right next to me.

We spent hours with each other,
talking drama, crashing out.
I don't think I would recover
if I lost what we have now.

I never asked for someone like you,
but I'm so thankful you're my friend,
and, though nothing's like it used to,
we'll be together till the end.

And now I know I shouldn't worry,

that even if I don't go back,

we won't forget this and we'll always

be best friends, no matter what.

4130 MILES

Inside my mind, I am still there,

feeling cold in a mid-western state.

A small town, not much to do,

smiling all my way to school.

I close my eyes, it's still November

all is white, I can remember,

feeling joyful, playing in snow…

I had never felt that young.

I go to sleep, I'm in those hallways,

hanging out around the lockers,

I go find her and, like always,

we tell each other all our problems.

And I'm so happy all the time,

even in class, I always smile.

"This place feels like something right,

I'd love to stay here all my life."

But it's all a fever dream,

just a memory of what has been,

cause I'm four thousand miles away

from that place and all my friends.

SIXTEEN

I turned sixteen today,

thought I'd leave you in the past,

but you'll never go away,

even if I'm growing up.

Plus, you texted me today,

saw it while I was in class.

I freaked out, wasn't okay.

Do you think you can do that?

You came back from out of nowhere,

I was trying to forget,

though I still miss you, and no less,

(you have never left my head).

But now you're there, like, all the time…

All I think about is you

and all that I can do is smile

because you may miss me, too.

Yeah, I turned sixteen today,

waited for your text all day.

Another year, but nothing changed:

I still love you, you don't care.

AKNOWLEDGEMENTS

If I'm being honest, writing "Rivers of Ink" was one of the most complicated experiences of my life. Not for the writing itself, but because, in order to feel all the things I wrote about, I had to put myself in the most complicated places I've ever been. Leaving my country, making new friends, falling in love, going back home… none of it was easy, and I am so thankful for all the people that walked this path by my side.

First of all, thank you to my family. Thank you to my parents, for letting me go all by myself to another country for five months, and for supporting me since the very beginning. Thank you to Fer, my brother and favorite person, for missing me all that time, for hating every guy I wrote a poem about and for sharing with me his basketball obsession, that has become a rather important part of my life. Te quiero muchísimo.

Secondly, thank you to my all friends here in Spain. Thank you especially to Andrea and Lola, who never failed to listen to my daily ten-minute podcasts about all of this and who have been my biggest fans since day 1. Thank you also to Ale, for becoming closer with my American friends than I am, and to Gabriel, for being my best friend and listening to all my voicemails ranting about boys.

Most importantly, thank you to all the people who made a small town in the middle of Wisconsin feel like home. Thank you to the Noltes, for taking care of me and including me in their family, and especially to Greta, for showing me what it's like to have an older sister. Thank you to all the teachers at FVL, who showed their care for me since the first day. Thank you to the internationals, to Linda, Claudia, Carla, Valeria, Carlota, Martí, and Sueun, for walking this journey by my side. Thank you to Addy for being the most incredible American friend I could've asked for; meeting you is one the best things that have ever happened to me and I still can't believe I've been lucky enough to find you.

Lastly, thank you to all my American friends: Caitlyn, Nora, Brianna, Ashley, Jocelyn, Paige, Anna, Lily, Natalie, Audrey, Alaina, Kayla, Alyvia, Estella, Eve, Claire, Belle, Camrynn, Gloria, Isla, Laura, Louisa, Jillian, Tabby, Andrea, Bella, Amari, Asher, Jake, Luke, Cael, Jose, Bryce, Brady, Jackson D, Landon, JJ, Grayson, Jackson K, Isaiah, Jack K, Levi, Kayden, Jack S, Jackson J, Braydon, Oliver, Rhody, Jaxson… Gracias. All of you made Appleton feel a little bit more special, and I'll never be able to express how much I owe you for that. I'll miss you forever and you'll always have a special place in my heart.

Finally, thank you to you, dear reader. Since the moment you picked this book up, all my feelings were yours. I hope that, at some point while reading this, you felt like you weren't alone. If you did, my job here is done. Thank you so much, for everything.